The Jewel Merchants

The Jewel Merchants

A Comedy in One Act

James Branch Cabell

MINT EDITIONS

The Jewel Merchants: A Comedy in One Act was first published in 1921.

This edition published by Mint Editions 2021.

ISBN 9781513295756 | E-ISBN 9781513297255

Published by Mint Editions®

MINT
EDITIONS
minteditionbooks.com

Publishing Director: Jennifer Newens
Design & Production: Rachel Lopez Metzger
Project Manager: Micaela Clark
Typesetting: Westchester Publishing Services

THE AUTHOR'S PROLOGUE

Prudence urges me here to forestall detection, by conceding that this brief play has no pretension to "literary" quality. It is a piece in its inception designed for, and in its making swayed by, the requirements of the little theatre stage. The one virtue which anybody anywhere could claim for *The Jewel Merchants* is the fact that it "acts" easily and rather effectively.

And candor compels the admission forthwith that the presence of this anchoritic merit in the wilderness is hardly due to me. When circumstances and the Little Theatre League of Richmond combined to bully me into contriving the dramatization of a short story called *Balthazar's Daughter*, I docilely converted this tale into a one-act play of which you will find hereinafter no sentence. The comedy I wrote is now at one with the lost dramaturgy of Pollio and of Posidippus, and is even less likely ever to be resurrected for mortal auditors.

It read, I still think, well enough: I am certain that, when we came to rehearse, the thing did not "act" at all, and that its dialogue, whatever its other graces, had the defect of being unspeakable. So at each rehearsal we—by which inclusive pronoun I would embrace the actors and the producing staff at large, and with especial (metaphorical) ardor Miss Louise Burleigh, who directed all—changed here a little, and there a little more; and shifted this bit, and deleted the other, and "tried out" everybody's suggestions generally, until we got at least the relief of witnessing at each rehearsal a different play. And steadily my manuscript was enriched with interlineations, to and beyond the verge of legibility, as steadily I substituted, for the speeches I had rewritten yesterday, the speeches which the actor (having perfectly in mind the gist but not the phrasing of what was meant) delivered naturally.

This process made, at all events, for what we in particular wanted, which was a play that the League could stage for half an evening's entertainment; but it left existent not a shred of the rhetorical fripperies which I had in the beginning concocted, and it made of the actual first public performance a collaboration with almost as many contributing authors as though the production had been a musical comedy.

And if only fate had gifted me with an exigent conscience and a turn for oratory, I would, I like to think, have publicly confessed, at that first public performance, to all those tributary clarifying rills to the play's progress: but, as it was, vainglory combined with an aversion to "speech-making" to compel a taciturn if smirking acceptance of the curtain-call with which an indulgent audience flustered the nominal author of *The Jewel Merchants*. . . Now, in any case, it is due my collaborators to tell you that *The Jewel Merchants* has amply fulfilled the purpose of its makers by being enacted to considerable applause,—and is a pleasure to add that this *succès d'estime* was very little chargeable to anything which I contributed to the play.

For another matter, I would here confess that *The Jewel Merchants*, in addition to its "literary" deficiencies, lacks moral fervor. It will, I trust, corrupt no reader irretrievably, to untraversable leagues beyond the last hope of redemption: but, even so, it is a frankly unethical performance. You must accept this resuscitated trio, if at all, very much as they actually went about Tuscany, in long ago discarded young flesh, when the one trait everywhere common to their milieu was the absence of any moral excitement over such-and-such an action's being or not being "wicked." This phenomenon of Renaissance life, as lived in Italy in particular, has elsewhere been discussed time and again, and I lack here the space, and the desire, either to explain or to apologize for the era's delinquencies. I would merely indicate that this point of conduct is the fulcrum of *The Jewel Merchants*.

The play presents three persons, to any one of whom the committing of murder or theft or adultery or any other suchlike interdicted feat, is just the risking of the penalty provided against the breaking of that especial law if you have the vile luck to be caught at it: and this to them is all that "wickedness" can mean. We nowadays are encouraged to think differently: but such dear privileges do not entitle us to ignore the truth that had any of these three advanced a dissenting code of conduct, it would, in the time and locality, have been in radical irreverence of the best-thought-of tenets. There was no generally recognized criminality in crime, but only a perceptible risk. So must this trio thriftily adhere to the accepted customs of their era, and regard an infraction of the Decalogue (for an instance) very much as we today look on a violation of our prohibition enactments.

In fact, we have accorded to the Eighteenth Amendment almost exactly the status then reserved for Omnipotence. You found yourself confronted by occasionally enforced if obviously unreasonable supernal statutory decrees, which every one broke now and then as a matter of convenience: and every now and then, also, somebody was caught and punished, either in this world or in the next, without his ill-fortune's involving any disgrace or particular reprehension. As has been finely said, righteousness and sinfulness were for the while "in strange and dreadful peace with each other. The wicked man did not dislike virtue, nor the good man vice: the villain could admire a saint, and the saint could excuse a villain, in things which we often shrink from repeating, and sometimes recoil from believing."

Such was the sixteenth-century Tuscan view of "wickedness." I have endeavored to reproduce it without comment.

So much of ink and paper and typography may be needed, I fear, to remind you, in a more exhortatory civilization, that Graciosa is really, by all the standards of her day, a well reared girl. To the prostitution of her body, whether with or without the assistance of an ecclesiastically acquired husband, she looks forward as unconcernedly as you must by ordinary glance out of your front window, to face a vista so familiar that the discovery of any change therein would be troubling. Meanwhile she wishes this sorrow-bringing Eglamore assassinated, as the obvious, the most convenient, and indeed the only way of getting rid of him: and toward the end of the play, alike for her and Guido, the presence of a corpse in her garden is merely an inconvenience without any touch of the gruesome. Precautions have, of course, to be taken to meet the emergency which has arisen: but in the dead body of a man *per se*, the lovers can detect nothing more appalling, or more to be shrunk from, than would be apparent if the lifeless object in the walkway were a dead flower. The thing ought to be removed, if only in the interest of tidiness, but there is no call to make a pother over it.

As for our Guido, he is best kept conformable to modern tastes, I suspect, by nobody's prying too closely into the earlier relations between the Duke and his handsome minion. The insistently curious may resort to history to learn at what price the favors of Duke Alessandro were secured and retained: it is no part of the play.

Above all, though, I must remind you that the Duke is unspurred by malevolence. A twinge of jealousy there may be, just at first, to find his pampered Eglamore so far advanced in the good graces of this pretty girl, but that is hardly important. Thereafter the Duke is breaking no law, for the large reason that his preference in any matter is the only law thus far divulged to him. As concerns the man and the girl he discovers on this hill-top, they, in common with all else in Tuscany, are possessions of Duke Alessandro's. They can raise no question as to how he "ought" to deal with them, for to your chattels, whether they be your finger rings or your subjects or your pomatum pots or the fair quires whereon you indite your verses, you cannot rationally be said to "owe" anything. . . No, the Duke is but a spirited lad in quest of amusement: and Guido and Graciosa are the playthings with which, on this fine sunlit morning, he attempts to divert himself.

This much being granted—and confessed,—we let the play begin.

Dumbarton Grange,
June, 1921

("Alessandro de Medici is generally styled by the Italian authors the first duke of Florence; but in this they are not strictly accurate. His title of duke was derived from Città, or Cività di Penna, and had been assumed by him several years before he obtained the direction of the Florentine state. It must also be observed, that, after the evasion of Eglamore, Duke Alessandro did not, as Robertson observes, 'enjoy the same absolute dominion as his family have retained to the present times,' (Hist. Charles V book v) he being only declared chief or prince of the republic, and his authority being in some measure counteracted or restrained by two councils chosen from the citizens, for life, one of which consisted of forty-eight, and the other of two hundred members. (Varchi, Storia Fior. p. 497: Nerli, Com. lib. xi. pp. 257, 264)")

Original Cast

Graciosa. . . . . .Elinor Fry
    Daughter of Balthazar Valori
Guido. . . . . .Roderick Maybee
    A jewel merchant
Alessandro De Medici. . . . . . . Francis F. Bierne
    Duke of Florence

Produced under the direction of Louise Burleigh.

The play begins with the sound of a woman's voice singing a song (adapted from Rossetti's version) which is delivered to the accompaniment of a lute.

Song:

> *Let me have dames and damsels richly clad*
> *To feed and tend my mirth,*
> *Singing by day and night to make me glad.*
>
> *Let me have fruitful gardens of great girth*
> *Filled with the strife of birds,*
> *With water-springs and beasts that house i' the earth.*
>
> *Let me seem Solomon for lore of words,*
> *Samson for strength, for beauty Absalom.*
>
> *Knights as my serfs be given;*
> *And as I will, let music go and come,*
> *Till, when I will, I will to enter Heaven.*

As the singing ends, the curtain rises upon a corner of Balthazar Valori's garden near the northern border of Tuscany. The garden is walled. There is a shrine in the wall: the tortured figure upon the crucifix is conspicuous. To the right stands a rather high-backed stone bench: by mounting from the seat to the top of the bench it is possible to scale the wall. To the left a crimson pennant on a pole shows against the sky. The period is 1533, and a few miles southward the Florentines, after three years of formally recognizing Jesus Christ as the sole lord and king of Florence, have lately altered matters as profoundly as was possible by electing Alessandro de Medici to be their Duke.

Graciosa is seated upon the bench, with a lute. The girl is, to our modern taste, very quaintly dressed in gold-colored satin, with a short tight bodice, cut square and low at the neck, and with long full skirts. When she stands erect, her preposterous "flowing" sleeves, lined with sky blue, reach to the ground. Her blonde hair, of which she has a great deal, is braided, in the intricate early sixteenth fashion, under a jeweled cap and a veil the exact color of this hair.

There is a call. Smiling, Graciosa answers this call by striking her lute. She pats straight her hair and gown, and puts aside the instrument. Guido appears at the top of the wall. All you can see of the handsome young fellow, in this posture, is that he wears a green skull-cap and a dark blue smock, the slashed sleeves of which are lined with green.

GUIDO: Ah, madonna. . .

GRACIOSA: Welcome, Ser Guido. Your journey has been brief.

GUIDO: It has not seemed brief to me.

GRACIOSA: Why, it was only three days ago you told me it would be a fortnight before you came this way again.

GUIDO: Yes, but I did not then know that each day spent apart from you, Madonna Graciosa, would be a century in passing.

GRACIOSA: Dear me, but your search must have been desperate!

GUIDO: (*Who speaks, as almost always hereinafter, with sober enjoyment of the fact that he is stating the exact truth unintelligibly*) Yes, my search is desperate.

GRACIOSA: Did you find gems worthy of your search?

GUIDO: Very certainly, since at my journey's end I find Madonna Graciosa, the chief jewel of Tuscany.

GRACIOSA: Such compliments, Guido, make your speech less like a merchant's than a courtier's.

GUIDO: Ah, well, to balance that, you will presently find courtiers in Florence who will barter for you like merchants. May I descend?

GRACIOSA: Yes, if you have something of interest to show me.

GUIDO: Am I to be welcomed merely for the sake of my gems? You were more gracious, you were more beautifully like your lovely name, on the fortunate day that I first encountered you. . . only six weeks ago, and only yonder, where the path crosses the highway. But now that I esteem myself your friend, you greet me like a stranger. You do not even invite me into your garden. I much prefer the manner in which you told me the way to the inn when I was an unknown passer-by. And yet your pennant promised greeting.

GRACIOSA: (*With the smile of an exceptionally candid angel*) Ah, Guido, I flew it the very minute the boy from the inn brought me your message!

GUIDO: Now, there is the greeting I had hoped for! But how do you escape your father's watch so easily?

GRACIOSA: My father has no need to watch me in this lonely hill castle. Ever since I can remember I have wandered at will in the forest. My father knows that to me every path is as familiar as one of the corridors in his house; and in no one of them did I ever meet anybody except charcoal-burners, and sometimes a nun from the convent, and—oh, yes!—you. But descend, friend Guido.

Thus encouraged, Guido *descends from the top of the wall to the top of the bench, and thence, via its seat, to the ground. You are thereby enabled to discover that his nether portions are clad in dark blue tights and soft leather shoes with pointed turned-up toes. It is also noticeable that he carries a jewel pack of purple, which, when opened, reveals an orange lining.*

Guido: (*With as much irony as the pleasure he takes in being again with this dear child permits*) That "Oh, yes, you!" is a very fitting reward for my devotion. For I find that nowadays I travel about the kingdom buying jewels less for my patrons at court than for the pleasure of having your eyes appraise them, and smile at me.

Graciosa: (*With the condescension of a great lady*) Guido, you have in point of fact been very kind to me, and very amusing, too, in my loneliness on the top of this hill. (*Drawing back the sleeve from her left arm, she reveals the trinket there*) See, here is the turquoise bracelet I had from you the second time you passed. I wear it always—secretly.

Guido: That is wise, for the turquoise is a talisman. They say that the woman who wears a turquoise is thereby assured of marrying the person whom she prefers.

Graciosa: I do not know about that, nor do I expect to have much choice as to what rich nobleman marries me, but I know that I love this bracelet—

Guido: In fact, they are handsome stones.

Graciosa: Because it reminds me constantly of the hours which I have spent here with my lute—

Guido: Oh, with your lute!

Graciosa: And with your pack of lovely jewels—

Guido: Yes, to be sure! with my jewels.

Graciosa: And with you.

Guido: There is again my gracious lady. Now, in reward for that, you shall feast your eyes.

Graciosa: (*All eagerness*) And what have you today?

Guido: *opens his pack. She bends above it with hands outstretched.*

Guido: (*Taking out a necklace*) For one thing, pearls, black pearls, set with a clasp of emeralds. See! They will become you.

Graciosa: (*Taking them, pressing them to her cheek*) How cool! But I— poor child of a poor noble—I cannot afford such.

Guido: Oh, I did not mean to offer them to you today. No, this string is intended for the Duke's favorite, Count Eglamore.

GRACIOSA: (*Stiffening*) Count Eglamore! These are for him?

GUIDO: For Count Eglamore.

GRACIOSA: Has the upstart such taste?

GUIDO: If it be taste to appreciate pearls, then the Duke's chief officer has excellent taste. He seeks them far and wide. He will be very generous in paying for this string.

GRACIOSA *drops the pearls, in which she no longer delights. She returns to the bench, and sits down and speaks with a sort of disappointment.*

GRACIOSA: I am sorry to learn that this Eglamore is among your patrons.

GUIDO: (*Still half engrossed by the contents of his pack. The man loves jewels equally for their value and their beauty*) Oh, the nobles complain of him, but we merchants have no quarrel with Eglamore. He buys too lavishly.

GRACIOSA: Do you think only of buying and selling, Guido?

GUIDO: It is a pursuit not limited to us who frankly live by sale and purchase. Count Eglamore, for example, knows that men may be bought as readily as merchandise. It is one reason why he is so hated—by the unbought.

GRACIOSA: (*Irritated by the title*) Count Eglamore, indeed! I ask in my prayers every night that some honest gentleman may contrive to cut the throat of this abominable creature.

GUIDO: (*His hand going to his throat*) You pray too much, madonna. Even very pious people ought to be reasonable.

GRACIOSA: (*Rising from the bench*) Have I not reason to hate the man who killed my kinsman?

GUIDO: (*Rising from his gems*) The Marquis of Cibo conspired, or so the court judged—

GRACIOSA: I know nothing of the judgment. But it was this Eglamore who discovered the plot, if there indeed was any plot, and who sent my cousin Cibo to a death—(*pointing to the shrine*)—oh, to a death as horrible as that. So I hate him.

GUIDO: Yet you have never even seen him, I believe?

GRACIOSA: And it would be better for him never to see me or any of my kin. My father, my uncles and my cousins have all sworn to kill him—

GUIDO: So I have gathered. They remain among the unbought.

GRACIOSA: (*Returning, sits upon the bench, and speaks regretfully*) But they have never any luck. Cousin Pietro contrived to have a beam dropped on Eglamore's head, and it missed him by not half a foot—

GUIDO: Ah, yes, I remember.

GRACIOSA: And Cousin Georgio stabbed him in the back one night, but the coward had on chain-armor under his finery—

GUIDO: I remember that also.

GRACIOSA: And Uncle Lorenzo poisoned his soup, but a pet dog got at it first. That was very unfortunate.

GUIDO: Yes, the dog seemed to think so, I remember.

GRACIOSA: However, perseverance is always rewarded. So I still hope that one or another of my kinsmen will contrive to kill this Eglamore before I go to court.

GUIDO: (*Sits at her feet*) Has my Lord Balthazar yet set a day for that presentation?

GRACIOSA: Not yet.

GUIDO: I wish to have this Eglamore's accounts all settled by that date.

GRACIOSA: But in three months, Guido, I shall be sixteen. My sisters went to court when they were sixteen.

GUIDO: In fact, a noble who is not rich cannot afford to continue supporting a daughter who is salable in marriage.

GRACIOSA: No, of course not. (*She speaks in the most matter-of-fact tone possible. Then, more impulsively, the girl slips down from the bench, and sits by him on the around*) Do you think I shall make as good a match as my sisters, Guido? Do you think some great rich nobleman will marry me very soon? And shall I like the court! What shall I see there?

GUIDO: Marvels. I think—yes, I am afraid that you will like them.

GRACIOSA: And Duke Alessandro—shall I like him?

GUIDO: Few courtiers have expressed dislike of him in my presence.

GRACIOSA: Do you like him? Does he too buy lavishly?

GUIDO: Eh, madonna! some day, when you have seen his jewels—

GRACIOSA: Oh! I shall see them when I go to court?

GUIDO: Yes, he will show them to you, I think, without fail, for the Duke loves beauty in all its forms. So he will take pleasure in confronting the brightness of your eyes with the brightness of the four kinds of sapphires, of the twelve kinds of rubies, and of many extraordinary pearls—

GRACIOSA: (*With eyes shining, and lips parted*) Oh!

GUIDO: And you will see his famous emerald necklace, and all his diamonds, and his huge turquoises, which will make you ashamed of your poor talisman—

GRACIOSA: He will show all these jewels to me!

GUIDO: (*Looking at her, and still smiling thoughtfully*) He will show you the very finest of his gems, assuredly. And then, worse still, he will be making verses in your honor.

GRACIOSA: It would be droll to have a great duke making songs about me!

GUIDO: It is a preposterous feature of Duke Alessandro's character that he is always making songs about some beautiful thing or another.

GRACIOSA: Such strange songs, Guido! I was singing over one of them just before you came,—

> *Let me have dames and damsels richly clad*
> *To feed and tend my mirth,*
> *Singing by day and night to make me glad—*

But I could not quite understand it. Are his songs thought good?

GUIDO: The songs of a reigning duke are always good.

GRACIOSA: And is he as handsome as people report?

GUIDO: Tastes differ, of course—

GRACIOSA: And is he—?

GUIDO: I have a portrait of the Duke. It does not, I think, unduly flatter him. Will you look at it?

GRACIOSA: Yes, yes!

GUIDO: (*Drawing out a miniature on a chain*) Here is the likeness.

GRACIOSA: But how should you—?

GUIDO: (*Seeing her surprise*) Oh, it was a gift to me from his highness for a special service I did him, and as such must be treasured.

GRACIOSA: Perhaps, then, I shall see yon at court, Messer Guido, who are the friend of princes?

GUIDO: If you do, I ask only that in noisy Florence you remember this quiet garden.

GRACIOSA: (*Looks at him silently, then glances at the portrait. She speaks with evident disappointment*) Is this the Duke?

GUIDO: You may see his arms on it, and on the back his inscription.

GRACIOSA: Yes, but—(*looking at the portrait again*)—but. . . he is. . . so. . .

GUIDO: You are astonished at his highness' coloring? That he inherits from his mother. She was, you know, a blackamoor.

GRACIOSA: And my sisters wrote me he was like a god!

GUIDO: Such observations are court etiquette.

GRACIOSA: (*With an outburst of disgust*) Take it back! Though how can you bear to look at it, far less to have it touching you! And only yesterday I was angry because I had not seen the Duke riding past!

GUIDO: Seen him! here! riding past!

GRACIOSA: Old Ursula told me that the Duke had gone by with twenty men, riding down toward the convent at the border. And I flung my sewing-bag straight at her head because she had not called me.

GUIDO: That was idle gossip, I fancy. The Duke rarely rides abroad without my—(*he stops*)—without my lavish patron Eglamore, the friend of all honest merchants.

GRACIOSA: But that abominable Eglamore may have been with him. I heard nothing to the contrary.

GUIDO: True, madonna, true. I had forgotten you did not see them.

GRACIOSA: No. What is he like, this Eglamore? Is he as appalling to look at as the Duke?

GUIDO: Madonna! but wise persons do not apply such adjectives to dukes. And wise persons do not criticize Count Eglamore's appearance, either, now that Eglamore is indispensable to the all-powerful Duke of Florence.

GRACIOSA: Indispensable?

GUIDO: It is thanks to the Eglamore whom you hate that the Duke has ample leisure to indulge in recreations which are reputed to be—curious.

GRACIOSA: I do not understand you, Guido.

GUIDO: That is perhaps quite as well. (*Attempting to explain as much as is decently expressible*) To be brief, madonna, business annoys the Duke.

GRACIOSA: Why?

GUIDO: It interferes with the pursuit of all the beautiful things he asks for in that song.

GRACIOSA: But how does that make Eglamore indispensable?

GUIDO: Eglamore is an industrious person who affixes seals, and signs treaties, and musters armies, and collects revenues, upon the whole, quite as efficiently as Alessandro would be capable of doing these things.

GRACIOSA: So Duke Alessandro merely makes verses?

GUIDO: And otherwise amuses himself as his inclinations prompt, while Eglamore rules Tuscany—and the Tuscans are none the worse off on account of it. (*He rises, and his hand goes to the dagger at his belt*) But is not that a horseman?

GRACIOSA: (*She too has risen, and is now standing on the bench, looking over the wall*) A solitary rider, far down by the convent, so far away that he seems hardly larger than a scarlet dragon-fly.

GUIDO: I confess I wish to run no risk of being found here, by your respected father or by your ingenious cousins and uncles.

GRACIOSA: (*She turns, but remains standing upon the bench*) I think your Duke is much more dangerous looking than any of them. Heigho! I can quite foresee that I shall never fall in love with this Duke.

GUIDO: A prince has means to overcome all obstacles.

GRACIOSA: No. It is unbefitting and a little cowardly for Duke Alessandro to shirk the duties of his station for verse-making and eternal pleasure-seeking. Now if I were Duke—

GUIDO: What would you do?

GRACIOSA: (*Posturing a little as she stands upon the bench*) If I were duke? Oh. . . I would grant my father a pension. . . and I would have Eglamore hanged. . . and I would purchase a new gown of silvery green—

GUIDO: In which you would be very ravishingly beautiful.

His tone has become rather ardent, and he is now standing nearer to her than the size of the garden necessitates. So GRACIOSA *demurely steps down from the bench, and sits at the far end.*

GRACIOSA: And that is all I can think of. What would you do if you were duke, Messer Guido?

GUIDO: (*Who is now sitting beside her at closer quarters than the length of the bench quite strictly demands*) I? What would I do if I were a great lord instead of a tradesman! (*Softly*) I think you know the answer, madonna.

GRACIOSA: Oh, you would make me your duchess, of course. That is quite understood. But I was speaking seriously, Guido.

GUIDO: And is it not a serious matter that a pedler of crystals should have dared to love a nobleman's daughter?

GRACIOSA: (*Delighted*) This is the first I have heard of it.

GUIDO: But you are perfectly right. It is not a serious matter. That I worship you is an affair which does not seriously concern any person save me in any way whatsoever. Yet I think that knowledge of the fact would put your father to the trouble of sharpening his dagger.

GRACIOSA: Ye-es. But not even Father would deny that you were showing excellent taste.

GUIDO: Indeed, I am not certain that I do worship you; for in order to adore whole-heartedly the idolater must believe his idol to be perfect. (*Taking her hand*) Now your nails are of an ugly shape, like that of little fans. Your nose is nothing to boast of. And your mouth is too large. I do not admire these faults, for faults they are undoubtedly—

GRACIOSA: Do they make me very ugly? I know that I have not a really good mouth, Guido, but do you think it is positively repulsive?

GUIDO: No. . . Then, too, I know that you are vain and self-seeking, and look forward contentedly to the time when your father will transfer his ownership of your physical attractions to that nobleman who offers the highest price for them.

GRACIOSA: But we daughters of the poor Valori are compelled to marry—suitably. We have only the choice between that and the convent yonder.

GUIDO: That is true, and nobody disputes it. Still, you participate in a monstrous bargain, and I would prefer to have you exhibit distaste for it.

Bending forward, GUIDO *draws from his jewel pack the string of pearls, and this he moodily contemplates, in order to evince his complete disinterestedness. The pose has its effect.* GRACIOSA *looks at him for a moment, rises, draws a deep breath, and speaks with a sort of humility.*

GRACIOSA: And to what end, Guido? What good would weeping do?

GUIDO: (*Smiling whimsically*) I am afraid that men do not always love according to the strict laws of logic. (*He drops the pearls, and, rising, follows her*) I desire your happiness above all things, yet to see you so abysmally untroubled by anything which troubles me is—another matter.

GRACIOSA: But I am not untroubled, Guido.

GUIDO: No?

GRACIOSA: No. (*Rather tremulously*) Sometimes I sit here dreading my life at court. I want never to leave my father's bleak house. I fear that I may not like the man who offers the highest price for me.

And it seems as if the court were a horrible painted animal, dressed in bright silks, and shining with jewels, and waiting to devour me.

Beyond the wall appears a hat of scarlet satin with a divided brim, which, rising, is revealed to surmount the head of an extraordinarily swarthy person, to whose dark skin much powder has only loaned the hue of death: his cheeks, however, are vividly carmined. This is all that the audience can now see of the young Duke *of* Florence, *whose proximity the two in the garden are just now too much engrossed to notice.*

The Duke *looks from one to the other. His eyes narrow, his teeth are displayed in a wide grin; he now understands the situation. He lowers his head as* Graciosa *moves.*

Graciosa: No, I am not untroubled. For I cannot fathom you, and that troubles me. I am very fond of you—and yet I do not trust you.

Guido: You know that I love you.

Graciosa: You tell me so. It pleases me to have you say it—

Guido: Madonna is candid this morning.

Graciosa: Yes, I am candid. It does please me. And I know that for the sake of seeing me you endanger your life, for if my father heard of our meetings here he would have you killed.

Guido: Would I incur such risks without caring?

Graciosa: No,—and yet, somehow, I do not believe it is altogether for me that you care.

The Duke *laughs.* Guido *starts, half drawing his dagger.* Graciosa *turns with an instinctive gesture of seeking protection. The* Duke's *head and shoulders appear above the wall.*

The Duke: And you will find, my friend, that the most charming women have just these awkward intuitions.

The Duke *ascends the wall, while the two stand motionless and silent. When he is on top of the wall,* Guido, *who now remembers that omnipotence perches there, makes haste to serve it, and obsequiously assists the* Duke *to descend. The* Duke *then comes well forward, in smiling meditation, and hands first his gloves, then his scarlet cloak (which you now perceive to be lined with ermine and sable in four stripes) to* Guido, *who takes them as a servant would attend his master.*

The removal of this cloak reveals the Duke *to be clad in a scarlet satin doublet, which has a high military collar and sleeves puffed with black. His tights also are of scarlet, and he wears shining soft black riding-boots. Jewels glisten at his neck. About his middle, too, there is a metallic gleaming, for he is equipped with a noticeably long sword and a dagger. Such is the personage who now addresses himself more explicitly to* GRACIOSA.

THE DUKE: (*Sitting upon the bench, very much at his ease while the others stand uncomfortably before him*) Yes, madonna, I suspect that Eglamore here cares greatly for the fact that you are Balthazar Valori's daughter, and cousin to the late Marquis of Cibo.

GRACIOSA: (*Just in bewilderment*) Eglamore!

THE DUKE: For Cibo left many kinsmen. These still resent the circumstance that the matching of his wits against Eglamore's wits earned for Cibo an unpleasantly public death-bed. So they pursue their feud against Eglamore with vexatious industry. And Eglamore goes about in hourly apprehension of another falling beam, another knife-thrust in the back, or another plate of poison.

GRACIOSA: (*She comprehends now*) Eglamore!

THE DUKE: (*Who is pleased alike by Eglamore's neat plan and by his own cleverness in unriddling it*) But if rich Eglamore should make a stolen match with you, your father—good thrifty man!—could be appeased without much trouble. Your cousins, those very angry but penniless Valori, would not stay over-obdurate to a kinsman who had at his disposal so many pensions and public offices. Honor would permit a truce with their new cousin Eglamore, a truce very profitable to everybody.

GRACIOSA: He said they must be bought somehow!

THE DUKE: Yes, Eglamore could bind them all to his interest within ten days. All could be bought at a stroke by marrying you. And Eglamore would be rid of the necessity of sleeping in chain-armor. Have I not unraveled the scheme correctly, Eglamore?

GUIDO: (*Smiling and deferential*) Your highness was never lacking in penetration.

GRACIOSA *at this, turns puzzled from one man to the other.*

GRACIOSA: Are you—?

THE DUKE: I am Alessandro de Medici, madonna.

GRACIOSA: The Duke!

THE DUKE: A sadly neglected prince, who wondered over the frequent absences of his chief counselor, and secretly set spies upon him. Eglamore here will attest as much—(*As* GRACIOSA *draws away from* GUIDO)—or if you cannot believe Eglamore any longer in anything, I shall have other witnesses within the half-hour. Yes, my twenty cut-throats are fetching back for me a brace of nuns from the convent yonder. I can imagine that, just now, my cut-throats will be in your opinion more trustworthy witnesses than is poor Eglamore. And my stout knaves will presently assure you that I am the Duke.

GUIDO: (*Suavely*) It happens that not a moment ago we were admiring your highness' portrait.

GRACIOSA: And so you are Count Eglamore. That is very strange. So it was the hand of Eglamore (*rubbing her hands as if to clean them*) that I touched just now. I thought it was the hand of my friend Guido. But I forget. There is no Guido. You are Eglamore. It is strange you should have been capable of so much wickedness, for to me you seem only a smirking and harmless lackey.

The DUKE is watching as if at a play. He is aesthetically pleased by the girl's anguish. GUIDO winces. As GRACIOSA begins again to speak, they turn facing her, so that to the audience the faces of both men are invisible.

GRACIOSA: And it was you who detected—so you said—the Marquis of Cibo's conspiracy. Tebaldeo was my cousin, Count Eglamore. I loved him. We were reared together. We used to play here in this garden. I remember how Tebaldeo once fetched me a wren's nest from that maple yonder. I stood just here. I was weeping, because I was afraid he would fall. If he had fallen, if he had been killed then, it would have been the luckier for him. They say that he conspired. I do not know. I only know that by your orders, Count Eglamore, my playmate Tebaldeo was fastened to a cross, like that (*pointing to the shrine*). I know that his arms and legs were each broken in two places with an iron bar. I know that this cross was then set upon a pivot, so that it turned slowly. I know that my dear Tebaldeo died very slowly in the sunlit marketplace, while the cross turned, and turned, and turned. I know this was a public holiday; the shopkeepers took holiday to watch him die, the boy who fetched me a wren's nest from yonder maple. And I know that you are Eglamore, who ordered these things done.

GUIDO: I gave orders for the Marquis of Cibo's execution, as was the duty of my office. I did not devise the manner of his punishment. The punishment for Cibo's crime was long ago fixed by our laws. All who attack the Duke's person must die thus.

GRACIOSA: (*Waves his excuses aside*) And then you plan this masquerade. You plan to make me care for you so greatly that even when I know you to be Count Eglamore I must still care for you. You plan to marry me, so as to placate Tebaldeo's kinsmen, so as to leave them—in your huckster's phrase—no longer unbought. It was a fine bold stroke of policy, I know, to use me as a stepping-stone to safety. But was it fair to me?

GUIDO: Graciosa. . . you shame me—

GRACIOSA: Look you, Count Eglamore, I was only a child, playing here, alone, and not unhappy. Oh, was it fair, was it worth while to match your skill against my ignorance?

THE DUKE: Fie, Donna Graciosa, you must not be too harsh with Eglamore—

GRACIOSA: Think how unhappy I would be if even now I loved you, and how I would loathe myself!

THE DUKE: It is his nature to scheme, and he weaves his plots as inevitably as the spider does her web—

GRACIOSA: But I am getting angry over nothing. Nothing has happened except that I have dreamed—of a Guido. And there is no Guido. There is only an Eglamore, a lackey in attendance upon his master.

THE DUKE: Believe me, it is wiser to forget this clever lackey—as I do—except when there is need of his services. I think that you have no more need to consider him—

He takes the girl's hand. GRACIOSA *now looks at him as though seeing him for the first time. She is vaguely frightened by this predatory beast, but in the main her emotion is as yet bewilderment.*

THE DUKE: For you are very beautiful, Graciosa. You are as slim as a lily, and more white. Your eyes are two purple mirrors in each of which I see a tiny image of Duke Alessandro. (GUIDO *takes a step forward, and the* DUKE *now addresses him affably*) Those nuns they are fetching me are big high-colored wenches with cheeks like apples. It is not desirable that women should be so large. Such women do not inspire a poet. Women should be little creatures that fear you. They should have thin plaintive voices, and in shrinking from you should be as slight to the touch as a cobweb. It is not possible to draw inspiration from a woman's beauty unless you comprehend how easy it would be to murder her.

GUIDO: (*Softly, without expression*) God, God!

The DUKE *looks with delight at* GRACIOSA, *who stands bewildered and childlike.*

THE DUKE: You fear me, do you not, Graciosa? Your hand is soft and cold as the skin of a viper. When I touch it you shudder. I am very tired of women who love me, of women who are infatuated by my beauty. You, I can see, are not infatuated. To you my touch will always be a martyrdom, you will always loathe me. And therefore I shall not weary of you for a long while, because the misery and the helplessness of my lovely victim will incite me to make very lovely verses.

He draws her to the bench, sitting beside her.

THE DUKE: Yes, Graciosa, you will inspire me. Your father shall have all the wealth and state that even his greedy imaginings can devise, so long as you can contrive to loathe me. We will find you a suitable husband—say, in Eglamore here. You shall have flattery and titles, gold and fine glass, soft stuffs and superb palaces and many lovely jewels—

The DUKE *glances down at the pedler's pack.*

THE DUKE: But Eglamore also has been wooing you with jewels. You must see mine, dear Graciosa.

GRACIOSA: (*Without expression*) Count Eglamore said that I must.

THE DUKE: (*Raises the necklace, and lets it drop contemptuously*) Oh, not such trumpery as this. I have in Florence gems which have not their fellows anywhere, gems which have not even a name, and the value of which is incalculable. I have jewels engendered by the thunder, jewels taken from the heart of the Arabian deer. I have jewels cut from the brain of a toad, and from the eyes of serpents. I have jewels which are authentically known to have fallen from the moon. Well, we will select the rarest, and have a pair of slippers encrusted with them, and in these slippers you shall dance for me, in a room that I know of—

GUIDO: (*Without moving*) Highness—!

THE DUKE: It will all be very amusing, for I think that she is now quite innocent, as pure as the high angels. Yes, it will be diverting to make her as I am. It will be an atrocious action that will inspire me to write lovelier verses than even I have ever written.

GUIDO: She is a child—

THE DUKE: Yes, yes, a frightened child who cannot speak, who stays as still as a lark that has been taken in a snare. Why, neither of her sisters can compare with this, and, besides, the elder one had a quite ugly mole upon her thigh—But that old rogue Balthazar Valori has a real jewel to offer, this time. Well, I will buy it.

GUIDO: Highness, I love this child—

THE DUKE: Ah, then you cannot ever be her husband. You would have suited otherwise. But we will find some other person of discretion—

For a moment the two men regard each other in silence. The DUKE *becomes aware that he is being opposed. His brows contract a little, but he rises from the bench rather as if in meditation than in anger. Then* GUIDO *drops the cloak and gloves he has been holding until this. His lackeyship is over.*

GUIDO: No!

THE DUKE: My friend, some long-faced people say you made a beast of me—

GUIDO: No, I will not have it.

THE DUKE: So do you beware lest the beast turn and rend you.

GUIDO: I have never been too nice to profit by your vices. I have taken my thrifty toll of abomination. I have stood by contentedly, not urging you on, yet never trying to stay you as you waded deeper and ever deeper into the filth of your debaucheries, because meanwhile you left me so much power.

THE DUKE: Would you reshape your handiwork more piously? Come, come, man, be content with it as I am. And be content with the kingdom I leave you to play with.

GUIDO: It was not altogether I who made of you a brainsick beast. But what you are is in part my handiwork. Nevertheless, you shall not harm this child.

THE DUKE: "Shall not" is a delightfully quaint expression. I only regret that you are not likely ever to use it to me again.

GUIDO: I know this means my ruin.

THE DUKE: Indeed, I must venture to remind you, Count Eglamore, that I am still a ruling prince—

GUIDO: That is nothing to me.

THE DUKE: And that, where you are master of very admirable sentiments, I happen to be master of all Tuscany.

GUIDO: At court you are the master. At your court in Florence I have seen many mothers raise the veil from their daughters' faces because you were passing. But here upon this hill-top I can see only the woman I love and the man who has insulted her.

THE DUKE: So all the world is changed, and Pandarus is transformed into Hector! Your words are very sonorous words, dear Eglamore, but by what deeds do you propose to back them?

GUIDO: By killing you, your highness.

THE DUKE: But in what manner? By stifling me with virtuous rhetoric? Hah, it is rather awkward for you—is it not—that our sumptuary laws forbid you merchants to carry swords?

GUIDO: (*Draws his dagger*) I think this knife will serve me, highness, to make earth a cleaner place.

THE DUKE: (*Drawing his long sword*) It would save trouble now to split you like a chicken for roasting. . . (*He shrugs, and sheathes his sword. He unbuckles his sword-belt, and lays it aside*) No, no, this farce ascends in interest. So let us play it fairly to the end. I risk nothing, since from this moment you are useless to me, my rebellious lackey—

GUIDO: You risk your life, for very certainly I mean to kill you.

THE DUKE: Two go to every bargain, my friend. Now, if I kill you, it is always diverting to kill; and if by any chance you should kill me, I shall at least be rid of the intolerable knowledge that tomorrow will be just like today.

He draws his dagger. The two men engage warily but with determination, the DUKE *presently advancing.* GUIDO *steps backward, and in the act trips over the pedler's pack, and falls prostrate. His dagger flies from his hand.* GRACIOSA, *with a little cry, has covered her face. Nobody strikes an attitude, because nobody is conscious of any need to be heroic, but there is a perceptible silence, which is broken by the* DUKE's *quiet voice.*

THE DUKE: Well! am I to be kept waiting forever? You were quicker in obeying my caprices yesterday. Get up, you muddy lout, and let us kill each other with some pretension of adroitness.

GUIDO: (*Rising, with a sob*) Ah!

He catches up the fallen dagger, and attacks the DUKE, *this time with utter disregard of the rules of fence and his own safety.* GUIDO *drives the* DUKE *back.* GUIDO *is careless of defence, and desirous only to kill. The* DUKE *is wounded, and falls with a cry at the foot of the shrine.* GUIDO *utters a sort of strangled growl. He raises his dagger, intending to hack at and mutilate his antagonist, who is now unconscious. As* GUIDO *stoops,* GRACIOSA, *from behind him, catches his arm.*

GRACIOSA: He gave you your life.

GUIDO *turns. He drops the weapon. He speaks with great gentleness, almost with weariness.*

GUIDO: Madonna, the Duke is not yet dead. That wound is nothing serious.

GRACIOSA: He spared your life.

GUIDO: It is impossible to let him live.

GRACIOSA: But I think he only voiced a caprice—

GUIDO: I think so, too, but I know that all this madman's whims are ruthless.

GRACIOSA: But you have power—

GUIDO: Power! I, who have attacked the Duke's person! I, who have done what your dead cousin merely planned to do!

GRACIOSA: Guido—!

GUIDO: Living, this brain-sick beast will make of you his plaything—and, a little later, his broken, soiled and cast-by plaything. It is therefore necessary that I kill Duke Alessandro.

GRACIOSA *moves away from him, and* GUIDO *rises.*

GRACIOSA: And afterward—and afterward you must die just as Tebaldeo died!

GUIDO: That is the law, madonna. But what he said is true. I am useless to him, a rebellious lackey to be punished. Whether I have his life or no, I am a lost man.

GRACIOSA: A moment since you were Count Eglamore, whom all our nobles feared—

GUIDO: Now there is not a beggar in the kingdom who would change lots with me. But at least I shall first kill this kingdom's lord.

He picks up his dagger.

GRACIOSA: You are a friendless and hunted man, in peril of a dreadful death. But even so, you are not penniless. These jewels here are of great value—

GUIDO *laughs, and hangs the pearls about her neck.*

GUIDO: Do you keep them, then.

GRACIOSA: There is a world outside this kingdom. You have only to make your way through the forest to be out of Tuscany.

GUIDO: (*Coolly reflective*) Perhaps I might escape, going north to Bologna, and then to Venice, which is at war with the Duke—

GRACIOSA: I can tell you the path to Bologna.

GUIDO: But first the Duke must die, because his death saves you.

GRACIOSA: No, Guido! I would have Eglamore go hence with hands as clean as possible.

GUIDO: Not even Eglamore would leave you at the mercy of this poet.

GRACIOSA: How does that matter! It is no secret that my father intends to market me as best suits his interests. And the great Duke of Florence, no less, would have been my purchaser! You heard him, "I will buy this jewel," he said. He would have paid thrice what any of my sisters' purchasers have paid. You know very well that my father would have been delighted.

GUIDO: (*Since the truth of what she has just said is known to him by more startling proofs than she dreams of, he speaks rather bitterly, as he sheathes the dagger*) And I must need upset the bargain between these jewel merchants!

GRACIOSA: (*Lightly*) "No, I will not have it!" Count Eglamore must cry. (*Her hand upon his arm*) My dear unthrifty pedler! it cost you a great deal to speak those words.

GUIDO: I had no choice. I love you. (*A pause. As* GRACIOSA *does not speak,* GUIDO *continues, very quiet at first*) It is a theme on which I shall not embroider. So long as I thought to use you as an instrument I could woo fluently enough. Today I saw that you were frightened and helpless—oh, quite helpless. And something in me changed. I knew for the first time that I loved you. And I knew I was not clean as you are clean. I knew that I had more in common with this beast here than I had with you.

GRACIOSA: (*Who with feminine practicality, while the man talks, has reached her decision*) We daughters of the Valori are so much merchandise. . . Heigho, since I cannot help it, since bought and sold I must be, one day or another, at least I will go at a noble price. Yet I do not think I am quite worth the wealth and power which you have given up because of me. So it will be necessary to make up the difference, dear, by loving you very much.

GUIDO *takes her hands, only half-believing that he understands her meaning. He puts an arm about her shoulder, holding her at a distance, the better to see her face.*

GUIDO: You, who had only scorn to give me when I was a kingdom's master! Would you go with me now that I am homeless and friendless?

GRACIOSA: (*Archly*) But to me you do not seem quite friendless.

GUIDO: Graciosa—!

GRACIOSA: And I doubt if you could ever find your way through the forest alone. (*But as she stands there with one hand raised to each of his shoulders her vindication is self-revealed, and she indicates her bracelet rather indignantly*) Besides, what else is a poor maid to do, when she is burdened with a talisman that compels her to marry the man whom she—so very much—prefers?

GUIDO: (*Drawing her to him*) Ah, you shall not regret that foolish preference.

GRACIOSA: But come! There is a path—(*They are gathering up the pack and its contents, as* GUIDO *pauses by the* DUKE) Is he—?

GUIDO: He will not enter Hell today. (*The* DUKE *stirs*) Already he revives, you see. So let us begone before his attendants come.

GUIDO *lifts her to the top of the wall. He lifts up the pack.*

GRACIOSA: My lute!

GUIDO: (*Giving it to her*) So we may pass for minstrels on the road to Venice.

GRACIOSA: Yes, singing the Duke's songs to pay our way. (GUIDO *climbs over the wall, and stands on the far side, examining the landscape beneath*) Horsemen!

GUIDO: The Duke's attendants fetching him new women—two more of those numerous damsels that his song demands. They will revive this ruinous songmaker to rule over Tuscany more foolishly than Eglamore governed when Eglamore was a great lord. (*He speaks pensively, still looking down*) It is a very rich and lovely country, this kingdom which a half-hour since lay in the hollow of my hand. Now I am empty-handed.

GRACIOSA: (*With mocking reproach*) Empty-handed!

She extends to him both her hands. GUIDO *takes them, and laughs joyously, saying, "Come!" as he lifts her down.*

There is a moment's silence, then is heard the song and lute-playing with which the play began, growing ever more distant: . . .

"Knights as my serfs be given;
And as I will, let music go and come."

. . . *The* DUKE *moves. The* DUKE *half raises himself at the foot of the crucifix.*

THE DUKE: Eglamore! I am hurt. Help me, Eglamore!

(THE CURTAIN FALLS)

A Note About the Author

James Branch Cabell (1879–1958) was an American writer of escapist and fantasy fiction. Born into a wealthy family in the state of Virginia, Cabell attended the College of William and Mary, where he graduated in 1898 following a brief personal scandal. His first stories began to be published, launching a productive decade in which Cabell's worked appeared in both *Harper's Monthly Magazine* and *The Saturday Evening Post*. Over the next forty years, Cabell would go on to publish fifty-two books, many of them novels and short-story collections. A friend, colleague, and inspiration to such writers as Ellen Glasgow, H.L. Mencken, Sinclair Lewis, and Theodore Dreiser, James Branch Cabell is remembered as an iconoclastic pioneer of fantasy literature.

A Note from the Publisher

Spanning many genres, from non-fiction essays to literature classics to children's books and lyric poetry, Mint Edition books showcase the master works of our time in a modern new package. The text is freshly typeset, is clean and easy to read, and features a new note about the author in each volume. Many books also include exclusive new introductory material. Every book boasts a striking new cover, which makes it as appropriate for collecting as it is for gift giving. Mint Edition books are only printed when a reader orders them, so natural resources are not wasted. We're proud that our books are never manufactured in excess and exist only in the exact quantity they need to be read and enjoyed.

bookfinity™

Discover more of your favorite classics with Bookfinity™.

- Track your reading with custom book lists.
- Get great book recommendations for your personalized Reader Type.
- Add reviews for your favorite books.
- AND MUCH MORE!

Visit **bookfinity.com** and take the fun Reader Type quiz to get started.

Enjoy our classic and modern companion pairings!

Classic & Modern

www.ingramcontent.com/pod-product-compliance
Lightning Source LLC
Chambersburg PA
CBHW020446030426
42337CB00014B/1429